ALASKA

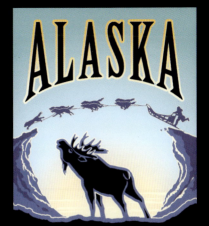

FACT AND TALL TALES

Edited and Compiled by Carrie Compton
Cover Illustration by Dave Ember

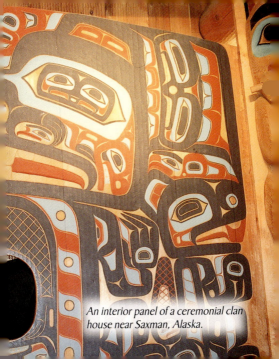

An interior panel of a ceremonial clan house near Saxman, Alaska.

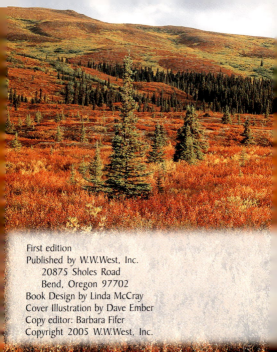

First edition
Published by W.W.West, Inc.
 20875 Sholes Road
 Bend, Oregon 97702
Book Design by Linda McCray
Cover Illustration by Dave Ember
Copy editor: Barbara Fifer
Copyright 2005 W.W.West, Inc.

Photographs copyright by photographer credited
ISBN 0-9727921-8-X
Printed in China by C & C Offset Printing Company
Effort has been made to attribute text to the original source. If any required credits have been omitted, or any rights overlooked, it is unintentional. Please notify the publisher and future editions will be corrected.

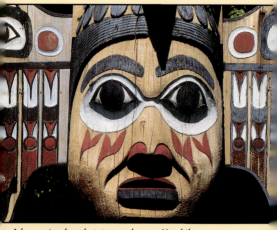

A humanized eagle totem pole near Ketchikan.

Alaska's First Peoples; Aleuts, Indians and Eskimos held a common belief of human and animal spirits being able to transform into new beings.

The slow pace of winter life encouraged artistic skills resulting in the creation of exceptional carvings, beautiful woven baskets and dramatic ceremonial masks.

An Eskimo skin mask.
A four-story-high totem at the Juneau City Museum.

A totem pole and clan house in Saxman Totem Park; Detail of totem.

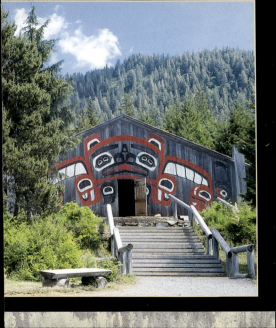

The traditions and artistic integrity of the native community have been born anew. Today, native artists and carvers produce work that is sought after by collectors of fine art. There is pride in performing everyday tasks as their ancestors once did.

Eskimo child with his handmade snowshoes.
Eskimo woman ice fishing.

They came to Alaska for adventure and riches. The wealth was found in soft-gold, real-gold and black-gold. First came the fur hunters and traders, followed by commercial fisherman.

Russians came for the "soft gold" of otter fur.

Gold discoveries created a frenzied rush of prospectors; and oil, perhaps 15 billion barrels, kept the adventurers coming to Alaska seeking their fortune.

The 800-mile pipeline transported Prudhoe Bay oil to Valdez on Prince William Sound.

Swanberg's Gold Dredge in Nome.

Salmon and halibut were the focus of Alaska's commercial fishing.

Oil tanker at sunset.

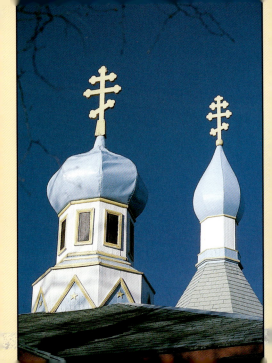

"Seward's Folly" editorial cartoonists, label for the 1885 Alaska purchase from Russia by William H. Seward, U.S. Secretary of State. Many leaders thought the U.S. acquired worthless, frozen and barren land. The price was $7.2 million; an amount equivalent to 2 cents per acre. Today, we realize the purchase of Alaska was an act of incredible foresight.

Holy Assumption Church was built in 1895.

"Nature always has something rare to show us."

John Muir

John Muir's writings about his 1879 Alaska adventure are credited with starting American tourist travel to Alaska. Tourism is now the economic engine of many Alaskan communities.

"Day after day, we seemed to float in a true fairyland, each succeeding view seeming more and more beautiful."

John Muir

Augustine Volcano at sunset.

Mendenhall Glacier, Juneau. Robin Brandt

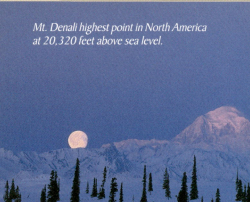
Mt. Denali highest point in North America at 20,320 feet above sea level.

The mountain is officially named Mt. McKinley. Denali, "The high one," is the Alaskan Athabaskan native name.

In 1906 a photograph of Frederick Cook on Mt. McKinley was hailed as proof of the first successful ascent to the top. Mr. Cook's remarkable climb was enthusiastically reported in the lower 48 states, but received with skepticism within Alaska.

The same Frederick Cook later proclaimed reaching the North Pole. Both claims were determined to be false.

Mt. McKinley was finally conquered in 1913 by a climbing party led by Hudson Stuck. Walter Harper, a member of the group and a native Alaskan, was the first person to reach the summit.

On June 6, 1947 Barbara Washburn was the first woman to climb to the top of Mt. McKinley.

Mount Sanford in Wrangell-St. Elias National Park

YUKON TERRITORY

KLUANE NATIONAL PARK

BRITISH COLUMBIA

- Frasier
- Skagway
- Haines
- Juneau

GLACIER BAY NATIONAL PARK

- Sitka

SITKA NATIONAL HISTORICAL PARK

MISTY FJORDS NATIONAL MONUMENT

- Ketchikan

Yes, Alaska is big. Alaskans enjoy the distinction of living in our largest state. A popular boast is, "If Alaska was split into two separate states, Texas would then be the third largest state."

- Alaska spans four time zones.

- The state encompasses 656,425 square miles, of which 571,951 square miles are land area.

- Over 28,000 square miles of glaciers.

- Including islands, there are 33,904 miles of shoreline.

- The National Park Service oversees an estimated 54 million acres in Alaska.

- Alaska is home of the nation's longest dog sled races, the Yukon Quest and the Iditarod.

Musher moving down the Yukon River during the Iditarod Trail Sled Dog Race. Kim Heacox

In the lower 48, March Madness is college basketball. In Alaska it is all about the Iditarod, which starts the first Saturday in March.

The Iditarod commemorates the January 1925 life saving delivery of diphtheria serum to Nome by relay teams of mushers. The course alternates yearly between a southern and northern route. Depending on the route, it is a 1,100- to 1,200-mile race.

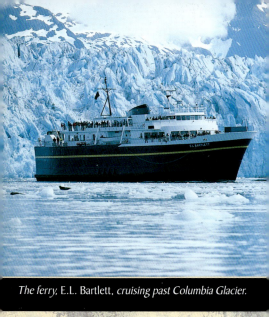

The ferry, E.L. Bartlett, *cruising past Columbia Glacier.*

Traveling Alaska may require using dog sleds, river boats, ferries, the railroad, or even float planes. Many Alaska communities do not have road access, including the state capital, Juneau.

Regardless of your transportation mode, it will be an adventure with spectacular scenery and wildlife all along the way.

The river boat Nenana Alaskaland docked in Fairbanks.

A brown bear greets a float plane arriving at Katmai Park. The Alaska railroad crossing over Riley Creek, Denali National Park.

Alaska has an abundance of mammals and birds. A huge land area with few people gives nature the chance to not only survive, but also to thrive. There are more grizzly bears and bald eagles in Alaska than in the rest of the United States.

"All things good are wild and free"

Henry David Thoreau

A moose is window shopping in Homer.

"The Last Frontier" is a nickname for the state, and its motto is "North to the Future." The future has already arrived. Alaska's population is growing rapidly. It is now the 47th state by population with 643,786 residents.

Anchorage is Alaska's largest city—population 268,983.

Front & Main Streets in Juneau. Robin Brandt

The Governor's Mansion in Juneau.
Robin Brandt

Summer weather forecast for Barrow, Alaska— "mostly sunny for the rest of the night."

24 hours each day, the summer daylight in Barrow exceeds 80 continuous days.

Polar bear in summer sunlight within the Arctic Circle.

The northern lights' formal name, Aurora borealis, combines Greek for "dawn" with Latin for "of the north."

Aurora borealis seen in Denali National Park.

Fairbanks is one of the best places to view the Northern Lights, and to see amazing ice sculptures during the World Championship of Ice Carving.

"If I were to name the three most precious resources of life, I should say books, friends and nature; and the greatest of these is nature."

John Burroughs

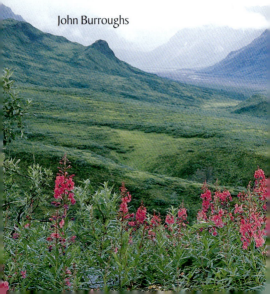

Sunrise on the Inside Passage.

"The sky, land, and water meet and blend in one inseparable scene of enchantment."

John Muir

South Sawyer Glacier.

Acknowledgments

Aleut—One of the three main groups of native peoples of Alaska. They lived primarily in the Aleutian Island Chain

Athabascan—an Indian tribe living mainly in the interior lands of Alaska.

John Burroughs (1837-1921) U.S. author, poet and naturalist.

Eskimo—the Inupiat Eskimo villages are grouped along the Bering Sea and the Arctic Circle. Yup'ik Eskimos live in southwestern Alaska.

Aldo Leopold (1887-1948) is considered the father of wildlife ecology. He is the author of the classic study, *A Sand County Almanac*.

John Muir (1838-1914) Conservationist, naturalist, author and explorer. He made several trips to Alaska and wrote *Travels in Alaska* in 1879.

William H. Seward (1801-1872) U.S. statesman and Secretary of State under presidents Lincoln and Andrew Johnson. He negotiated the purchase of Alaska from Russia.

Henry David Thoreau (1817-1862) U.S. philosopher and author whose work reflected his love of nature.

Mark Twain (1835-1919) U.S. author of such classic stories as *Tom Sawyer* and *Innocents Abroad*.

The totem is an icon of the native peoples of southeastern Alaska.